MW01676283

**American Civics**

# The Congress of the United States

**by David Heath**

**Consultant:**
Steven S. Smith,
Distinguished McKnight University
Professor of Political Science,
University of Minnesota

CAPSTONE
HIGH/LOW BOOKS
an imprint of Capstone Press
Mankato, Minnesota

Capstone High/Low Books are published by Capstone Press
818 North Willow Street • Mankato, Minnesota 56001
http://www.capstone-press.com


Printed in the United States of America.

*Library of Congress Cataloging-in-Publication Data*
Heath, David, 1948–
The Congress of the United States/by David Heath.
p. cm.—(American civics)
Includes bibliographical references and index.
Summary: Discusses the history and structure of the two branches of Congress and how they make laws.
ISBN 0-7368-0001-8
1. United States. Congress—Juvenile literature. [1. United States. Congress.] I. Title. II. Series.
JK1025.H43 1999
328.73'079—dc21 98-18224
CIP
AC

**Editorial Credits**
Colleen Sexton, editor; Timothy Halldin, cover designer and illustrator; Sheri Gosewisch, photo researcher

**Photo Credits**
Archive Photos, 30
Capstone Archives, cover
Corbis-Bettmann, 36
Reuters/Archive Photos/Win McNamee, 5; Ho, 26; Gary Hershorn, 46
Shaffer Photography/James L. Shaffer, 10
Uniphoto, 13
UPI/Corbis-Bettmann, 18, 21, 23, 29, 38, 41, 43
U.S. Capitol Historical Society, 9, 35
Visuals Unlimited/Bruce Berg, 33
William B. Folsom, 6

# Table of Contents

# Fast Facts about the U.S. Congress

**Number of Houses:** Two

**Names of Houses:** The House of Representatives and the Senate

**Location:** U.S. Capitol, Washington, D.C.

**Number of Members:** House of Representatives—435; Senate—100

**Terms of Office:** Representative—two years; Senator—six years

**Minimum Ages:** Representative—25; Senator—30

**Presiding Officers:** House of Representatives—Speaker of the House; Senate—Vice President of the United States

**Main Duty:** Make federal laws

**Members of the U.S. Congress make federal laws.**

We the People of the United States

## Chapter 1

# Congress

The U.S. government has three branches. They are the legislative branch, the executive branch, and the judicial branch.

Congress is part of the legislative branch. Congress makes laws for the country. The president leads the executive branch. This branch carries out U.S. laws. The Supreme Court is part of the judicial branch. This branch makes sure all laws agree with the U.S. Constitution.

The U.S. Constitution is the basis of the U.S. government. This document explains how the three branches of government operate. It also states the rights of citizens. The Constitution was approved in 1789.

**The U.S. Constitution is the basis of the U.S. government.**

## The Senate and the House of Representatives

The Constitution explains how Congress works. Congress consists of two parts called houses. The two houses are the House of Representatives and the Senate. Each house has many members. The Constitution explains who can be a member of each house.

The House of Representatives has 435 members called representatives. Each member represents an area of a state called a congressional district. The number of congressional districts in each state depends on the state's population. States with larger populations have more congressional districts than states with smaller populations. Each state has at least one congressional district.

Members of the House of Representatives must be at least 25 years old. Each representative must have been a U.S. citizen for at least seven years. Representatives also must live in the states they represent. Representatives hold office for two-year terms. All representatives begin and end their terms at the same time.

**The House of Representatives has 435 members.**

The Senate has 100 members called senators. Two senators represent each of the 50 states. Senators hold office for six-year terms. Voters do not elect all the senators at the same time. One-third of the Senate comes up for election every two years.

The Constitution states the requirements needed to be a senator. Senators must be at least 30 years old. Senators must have been

**New U.S. citizens take the oath of citizenship. Congress makes rules for becoming a U.S. citizen.**

U.S. citizens for at least nine years. Senators also must live in the states they represent.

## The Powers of Congress

The Constitution outlines the powers of Congress. The most important power of Congress is to make laws for the United States. Another important power is to make rules for becoming a U.S. citizen.

Congress has the power to govern trade. Congress controls trade between states and between the United States and other countries.

Congress approves the coining of money and oversees the collection of taxes. Tax money pays the costs of running the government. It also pays for programs that help citizens. Congress can borrow money if the government needs additional funds.

The Constitution gives Congress the power to set up and maintain military forces. Congress also has the power to declare war on other countries.

## Special Duties and Powers

The Constitution gives each house of Congress some special duties and powers. All bills about taxes and other money earned by the government start in the House. A bill is a plan for a new law. Impeachment proceedings also begin in the House. Impeach means to remove a public official from office.

The Senate holds trials for impeachments. The Senate approves the people the president appoints to certain positions. The Senate approves all treaties between the United States and other countries. Treaties create formal agreements between countries.

## Political Parties

Senators and representatives belong to political parties. A political party is a group that holds certain beliefs about government and important issues. The largest parties in the United States are the Democratic Party and the Republican Party. The party that has the majority of members in each house has certain advantages.

The leader of the House of Representatives comes from the majority party. This representative is the Speaker of the House. Representatives elect the Speaker. The Speaker is one of the most powerful people in Congress. The Speaker leads the business of the House and can favor certain bills. The Speaker decides the order in which bills will be discussed in the House.

The vice president of the United States leads the Senate. But members of the Senate also

**Members of Congress meet in committees to write and discuss bills.**

choose a majority leader. The majority leader is the most powerful senator. The majority leader schedules the order in which the Senate votes on bills.

In both houses, the majority party chooses a chairperson for each committee. A committee is a small group of senators or representatives that writes and discusses bills. The committee chairperson leads the meetings and plans the committee's schedule.

# How a Bill Becomes a Law

A bill must pass through many steps to become a law.
This illustration shows how two bills might go through the lawmaking process.

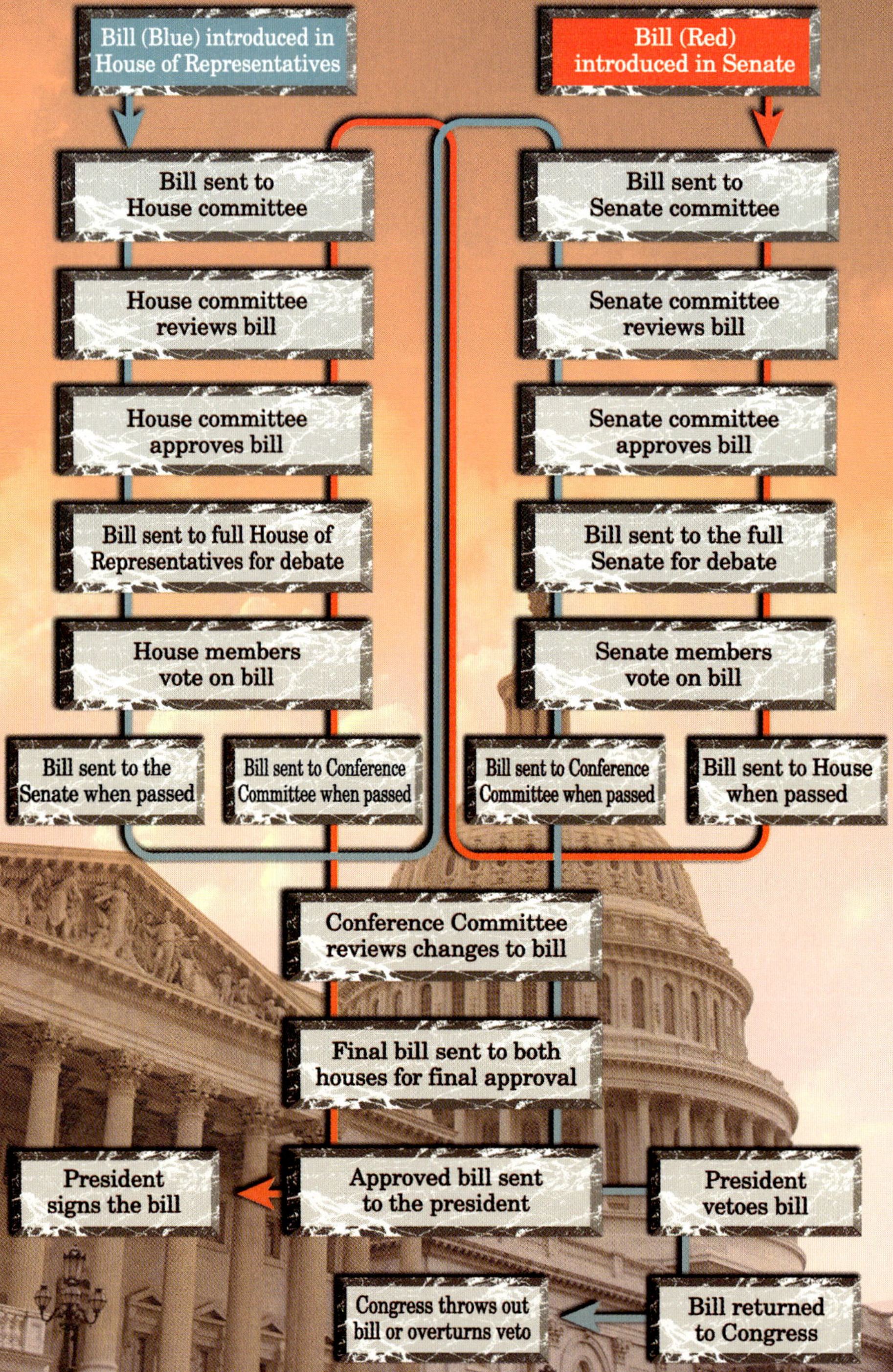

Chapter 2

# How Congress Makes Laws

Congress works on about 20,000 bills each year. Only about 2,000 of these bills become laws. It is not easy for a bill to become a law. A bill must first pass through many steps.

## How a Bill Becomes a Law

Anyone can have an idea for a new law. But the idea must be introduced as a bill by a member of Congress. Most bills start in either the Senate or the House of Representatives. Each bill goes through the same steps no matter which house begins the process. Members of Congress can delay, stop, or change a bill at any step.

For example, a representative introduces a new bill in the House. The bill then goes to one of the House committees. Each House committee has a special area of interest. For example, the Armed Services Committee studies bills about the military.

The committee holds meetings to discuss the bill. The committee sometimes holds hearings to gather facts. Experts present facts at the hearings. The committee often changes the bill. The committee sometimes votes to stop the bill.

The bill goes back to the full House if the committee approves it. Representatives debate the bill on the House floor. They present opposing views of the bill during their debate. Representatives sometimes decide to send a bill back to the committee for more changes. Representatives might make changes to the bill before they pass it. The bill also could pass with no changes.

The bill goes to the Senate after it passes in the House. The Senate sends the bill to a Senate committee. This committee works in the same way as the House committee.

The bill goes back to the entire Senate if the committee approves it. The whole Senate debates the bill. The bill goes to a special conference committee if the Senate wants to change it.

Members of both the Senate and the House are on the conference committee. They discuss the changes the Senate has made to the bill. The conference committee rewrites the bill until everyone agrees. The bill then goes back to the House and the Senate for a vote.

The bill goes to the president to sign if both the House and Senate pass the bill. The bill becomes a law if the president signs it.

### Presidential Veto

The president may disagree with the bill. The president has the power to veto it. The president's veto stops a bill from becoming a law.

A bill goes back to Congress if the president vetoes it. Congress can still make the bill a law. Two-thirds of each house of Congress must vote to approve the bill. It takes that many votes to overturn the president's veto. The bill then becomes a law. The bill does not become a law if Congress cannot overturn the president's veto.

Chapter 3

# Checks and Balances

The writers of the U.S. Constitution believed no branch of government should have more power than another. This system is called separation of powers. Each branch has specific duties. The way the branches work together is called the system of checks and balances. In this system, each branch checks the work of the other branches. These checks give each branch equal power.

## Congress and the President

The president works with Congress in many ways. The president sends ideas for bills to Congress. Members of Congress may put the president's ideas into bills and introduce them

**President Harry S. Truman meets with members of Congress in 1951.**

in one of the houses. The bills then go through the lawmaking process.

The president reviews all bills passed by Congress. The president can either sign the bills into law or veto them. But Congress has the power to overturn the president's veto. In this way, the president and Congress check each other's work.

The president and Congress work together on the government's budget. The budget is a plan for how the government will earn and spend money. The president creates a budget and sends it to Congress. Congress must approve the budget before the government can spend tax money. Congress sometimes makes changes to the budget. The budget is approved when the president and Congress agree.

The Senate screens people the president chooses for important jobs. The Senate either approves or rejects cabinet members, Supreme Court justices, and ambassadors. Cabinet members lead departments in the executive branch. They advise the president about

**President Franklin D. Roosevelt signs a bill into law. The president reviews all bills passed by Congress.**

important issues. Supreme Court justices hear cases in the nation's highest court. Ambassadors are people who represent the United States in foreign countries.

The president has the power to make treaties with other countries. But the Senate must approve any treaty the president makes. The Senate makes sure the treaty is in the best interest of the United States.

Congress also has the power to impeach the president. Congress can impeach presidents who break the law or neglect their duties. The House begins impeachment proceedings. The Senate holds impeachment trials.

### Congress and the Supreme Court

The Supreme Court decides if laws agree with the Constitution. Justices have the power to overturn laws by declaring them unconstitutional. In this way, the Supreme Court checks the work of Congress.

Congress also checks the work of the Supreme Court. The Senate must approve new Supreme Court justices. The Senate makes sure new justices are qualified for the job. Senators question justices to make certain they will be fair. A Supreme Court justice must look at all sides of an issue before making a decision.

Congress has powers that relate to the judicial branch. Congress has the power to set up new federal courts when they are needed. Congress also can impeach Supreme Court justices.

**Sandra Day O'Connor is sworn in as a justice. The Senate must approve all Supreme Court appointments.**

## Chapter 4

# A Day in Congress

No two days are exactly the same for members of Congress. They work at the U.S. Capitol in Washington, D.C., when Congress is in session. Members also work in offices in the states they represent. They talk to people in their congressional districts. Members of Congress find out what people in their home states think about upcoming bills. They also find out what types of laws people need.

### Early Morning

Members of Congress start work at home early in the morning. They usually read the newspaper and watch the morning news on TV. Members of Congress sometimes appear on morning news shows to discuss their opinions on important issues.

**Members of Congress work at the U.S. Capitol.**

**Senators Trent Lott and Tom Daschle appear on a morning news program.**

Members review their calendar of events for the day. They may read their notes about upcoming bills. Or they may study bills they will discuss in committee meetings. Members also check in with their offices in their home states. They then head to work at the U.S. Capitol.

## Late Morning

At their offices, members of Congress meet with their staffs. Together, they discuss new bills that members of Congress will present. Staff members also may discuss research for other bills currently being debated in committees. Staff members research important points to include in bills.

Members of Congress read their mail and make notes. Staff members answer most letters. Members of Congress also read their e-mail messages and return phone calls. They may call other members of Congress to discuss important points about bills in committees.

Members of Congress gather in large meeting rooms called chambers to discuss important issues. Each house has its own chamber. Members have the opportunity to speak about each bill scheduled for that day. They vote on each bill after a discussion. Large, lighted boards show how each member votes.

Members of Congress usually have lunch meetings. They may meet with other members of Congress or with constituents. Constituents live and vote in a member's home state or district. Members also may meet with reporters to explain their votes on certain bills. Members also tell reporters their ideas about important issues.

## The Afternoon

Members of Congress may attend committee meetings in the afternoon. Members are assigned to committees based on their experience and their party. At committee meetings, they may give speeches that explain their thoughts about bills.

Members may spend some time in their offices talking to staff members about that day's events. Members of Congress make phone calls to one another about upcoming votes. Members also review newsletters or announcements that will go to people in their home state.

## The Evening

Members of Congress often work in the evenings. They give speeches about issues to political groups or business groups.

Members of Congress also meet with business groups from their home states. Many of these groups lobby members. Lobbyists try to convince government officials to vote a certain way. Members of Congress and

**Members of Congress sometimes attend receptions in the evenings.**

lobbyists discuss new laws. Lobbyists want Congress to pass laws that will favor businesses or other groups they represent.

Members of Congress sometimes attend receptions in the evening. These formal gatherings might be held to welcome officials from other countries. Or they might be held to honor people such as military heroes or teachers.

## Chapter 5

# The U.S. Capitol

Congress has held sessions in the U.S. Capitol in Washington, D.C., since 1800. The British army burned the building in 1814 during the War of 1812 (1812–1814). Workers finished rebuilding the Capitol in 1830.

Workers added to the Capitol as more states joined the nation. Senators and representatives from these new states needed offices and meeting rooms. Workers built a new wing for the House in 1857. Senators moved into another new wing in 1859.

Today, the Capitol does not have enough offices for all the members of Congress and their staffs. Some senators and representatives have offices in six large buildings near the Capitol.

**The U.S. Capitol stands in Washington, D.C. Congress has met in the Capitol since 1800.**

## The Capitol Building

The Capitol has not changed much on the outside since it was completed in 1859. Pictures from a century ago show that the building looks the same today as it did then.

The Capitol stands at one end of the National Mall. The National Mall is a grassy area bordered by museums and monuments. The place where the Capitol stands is sometimes called Capitol Hill.

The Capitol is a large building with about 540 rooms. It covers about four acres (1.6 hectares). The building is more than 751 feet (229 meters) long. It stands 288 feet (88 meters) tall.

A huge dome made of iron and stone rises above the main building. The Statue of Freedom stands on top of the dome. The statue is a woman in flowing robes holding a sword and a shield. The statue stands for freedom in the United States during both war and peace.

**The main entrance of the Capitol leads into the rotunda.**

## Inside the Capitol

The main entrance to the Capitol leads into a large, round room called the rotunda. The rotunda is directly under the dome. The room has marble floors and artwork. Statues and paintings show people and scenes from U.S. history.

The National Statuary Hall is near the rotunda. Each state sent two statues to be displayed in the room in 1864. The statues are figures of important people from each state.

Many more states had joined the country by the 1930s. So there was not enough room in the hall for all the statues. Some statues are on display in other parts of the Capitol today.

### The Wings

Each house of Congress has its own wing in the Capitol. The chambers for both houses are located in these wings.

The Senate Chamber has many rows of individual desks set up in a half-circle. Each senator sits at a desk that faces a low platform. The vice president sits on this platform. Members of the Republican Party sit to the vice president's left. Democrats sit to the vice president's right.

Builders decorated the Senate Chamber with dark wood. Statues of 20 vice presidents are displayed around the chamber.

The House Chamber is officially called the Hall of the House of Representatives. It is set up the same way as the Senate Chamber. But representatives sit at long benches instead of desks. The House Chamber also is larger because it must hold more people.

**Senators meet in the Senate Chamber.**

The Speaker of the House sits on a platform facing the representatives. Representatives sit with their parties on opposite sides of the chamber.

The House Chamber also has dark wood. Paintings of important lawmakers decorate the walls. A decorated rod called a mace stands to the right of the Speaker when the House is in session. The mace stands for authority.

Visitors sit in viewing galleries in both chambers. The viewing galleries are balconies on the third floor. From there, visitors can watch and listen to Congress in session.

Chapter 6

# The History of Congress

The first Congress under the U.S. Constitution met on March 4, 1789, in New York City. Congress then had 20 senators and 59 representatives. Congress also met in Philadelphia before moving to Washington, D.C., in 1800.

## The 1800s

Slavery was the biggest issue facing Congress during the 1800s. Congress passed many laws about slavery. Congress also debated the rights of slaves. Members of Congress often disagreed.

The Civil War (1861–1865) divided the nation and Congress. Eleven states withdrew from the country. Southern states formed their own government. Many members left Congress.

**The first Congress met in 1789 in New York City.**

**In 1920, Congress changed the U.S. Constitution to give women the right to vote.**

Southern states rejoined the United States after the Civil War. Southerners again were elected to Congress. Congress outlawed slavery in 1865. Members of Congress changed the Constitution to allow African American men to vote. Congress also made many laws to help the United States rebuild areas damaged during the war. Congress passed laws to rebuild the country's economy.

Congress passed many laws about business and trade during the 1800s. Congress made laws to help farmers and to expand the railroad system. These laws allowed farmers and businesses to transport goods more easily.

### The 1900s

In 1917, Congress voted to send troops to Europe to fight in World War I (1914–1918). When the war ended, the Senate did not approve the peace treaty. Part of the treaty called for countries to form the League of Nations.

The League of Nations would consist of many countries that would work together on world issues. Congress did not want the United States to be part of this organization. Congress did not want the League of Nations to give orders to the United States. Other countries formed the League of Nations. But the United States did not join.

In 1920, Congress changed the Constitution to give women the right to vote. Women had worked many years to show lawmakers that women deserved the right to vote.

The Great Depression struck the United States in 1929. The United States experienced hard times. Millions of people lost their jobs and many became homeless. Congress passed hundreds of new laws between 1930 and 1941. These laws provided help to people who did not have jobs.

Congress created Social Security and other programs in the 1930s. Social Security is a program that U.S. workers pay into. The program provides money for older people and for people who are disabled.

Congress declared war again in 1941. U.S. troops fought in World War II (1939–1945) in Europe, Asia, and other parts of the world.

Civil rights became a major issue for Congress after the war. Civil rights are the rights given to citizens by the law. African Americans wanted the same rights as other U.S. citizens. Congress passed several civil rights bills. These laws gave all citizens equal rights to vote and to be treated fairly in jobs.

## Recent Years

The Vietnam War (1954–1975) caused strong disagreements in Congress. This war was between North Vietnam and South Vietnam. Congress did not declare this war. But the president sent troops

**Congress entered the United States in World War II in 1941.**

to help the South Vietnamese. Many people were against U.S. involvement in this war. They wanted Congress to bring troops home. But Congress did not have the power to stop the war.

Congress has worked mainly on economic issues since the mid-1970s. Some people think the government should not control businesses. Other people want the government to make laws that control businesses. Congress has worked to find a balance between these two sides.

# Words to Know

**bill** (BIL)—a plan for a new law

**budget** (BUHJ-it)—a plan for how the government will earn and spend money

**chamber** (CHAYM-bur)—a large meeting room

**committee** (kuh-MIT-ee)—a small group of senators or representatives formed to write and discuss bills

**constituents** (kuhn-STIHT-choo-ehnts)—the people who live and vote in a Congress member's home state or district

**impeach** (im-PEECH)—to remove a public official from office

**lobby** (LAH-bee)—to try to convince a government official to vote a certain way

**political party** (puh-LIT-ih-kuhl PAR-tee)—a group that holds certain beliefs about government and important issues

**veto** (VEE-toh)—to stop a bill from becoming a law

**Members of Congress take the oath of office.**

# To Learn More


**Judson, Karen.** *The Constitution of the United States.* American Government in Action. Springfield, N.J.: Enslow Publishers, 1996.

**Kronenwetter, Michael.** *The Congress of the United States.* American Government in Action. Springfield, N.J.: Enslow Publishers, 1996.

**Santella, Andrew.** *The Capitol.* Cornerstones of Freedom. Chicago: Children's Press, 1995.

**Stein, R. Conrad.** *The Powers of Congress.* Cornerstones of Freedom. Chicago: Children's Press, 1995.

**Weber, Michael.** *Our Congress.* I Know America. Brookfield, Conn.: Millbrook Press, 1994.

# Useful Addresses

**Library of Congress**
101 Independence Avenue SE
Washington, DC 20540

**United States House of Representatives**
Washington, DC 20515

**United States Senate**
Washington, DC 20510

# Internet Sites

**Congressional Leadership**
http://www.vote-smart.org/reference/primer/clead.html

**C-Span**
http://www.cspan.org

**How a Bill Becomes a Law**
http://www.vote-smart.org/reference/primer/billlaw.html

**The U.S. House of Representatives**
http://www.house.gov

**The U.S. Senate**
http://www.senate.gov

**A Virtual Tour of the Capitol**
http://www.senate.gov/about/capitol/virtour.html

**Members of Congress attend inauguration ceremonies at the U.S. Capitol. Presidents take the oath of office during these ceremonies.**

# Index